D0359011

David Livingstone
Who is the Bravest?

The true story of David Livingstone and his journeys

Catherine Mackenzie
Illustrated by Rita Ammassari

David Livingstone lived in the little town of Blantyre, in Scotland. He often went exploring in order to find out about animals and plants and other interesting things.

David was very hard working and had to work all day in the local mill. He was clever too as he read books whenever he could. David was also brave. One time he jumped into the river to save a little boy who was drowning.

David was also brave.

But David did not always feel happy. He wanted to have peace with God and didn't know how to get it. Then one day David realised that God loved him. God would forgive David for the wrong things he had done if David trusted in God's Son, Jesus Christ. David knew that Jesus had died on the cross to save him from sin. "Jesus is the bravest one of all," thought David.

David realised that God loved him.

One day an old man told David about Africa, where many thousands of people had never heard the name of Jesus. David trained to be a doctor and then a preacher so that he could go and tell the people there about Jesus.

When David set off for Africa he was glad to be going – but he was anxious too.

"It isn't always easy being brave," thought David. "But God is with me. He'll be in Africa too."

David set off for Africa.

There were lots of jungles and rivers to explore. David discovered waterfalls and mountains in Africa. He learned the African language. Everywhere he went David told the people about how God forgives sin.

David knew that even in the most dangerous jungle Jesus Christ was with him. David could trust in him.

"He makes me brave and he gives me strength," David smiled. "Thank you God."

David learned the African
language.

David felt lonely sometimes though. His family was far away and letters took a long time to arrive. He was often in danger and was even attacked by a lion. But David fought back and with the help of his friends he killed the lion. God kept him safe.

Some time later David married a young woman called Mary.

"It's good not to feel lonely any more," he said smiling.

David fought back and killed the lion.

David and Mary worked hard together. They set up schools and taught people about God. They travelled on wagons to find new places where the people needed their help. When they crossed the Kalahari Desert their children came with them. The whole family needed to be brave now.

But when they ran out of water the children became very ill. David decided to send them back to the United Kingdom with their mother. He would continue the work on his own.

David and Mary worked hard
together.

David's family had to be brave without their father. And David had to be brave without them. He missed them so much. But he knew he had to keep going. David's work was important.

If he could find a place with lots of rivers and people then that would be a good place to build a mission. Other missionaries would come and many more Africans would hear about the one true God who loved them.

David's work was important.

It was difficult for David without his family. It was dangerous travelling in Africa. Lions and hippos attacked him and then there were mosquitoes, diseases, droughts and famine. David was often sick, hungry and thirsty.

But God gave David the courage and the strength to do what needed to be done.

It was dangerous travelling in Africa.

After five years away from his family David finally went back to the United Kingdom. Mary was overjoyed to see her husband. When he was well enough to go back to Africa she went with him.

However, it wasn't long before Mary fell sick and died. David was on his own again, but he carried on with his work. David knew that he wasn't really alone.

"My God is with me now just as he has always been."

David knew that he wasn't really alone.

David travelled far and wide, discovering new rivers and jungles, waterfalls and villages. He travelled so far in fact that nobody knew where to find him.

Mr Stanley, an American journalist, went out to search for him. When he found him he tried to persuade David to return home to visit his children.

But David knew that God had work for him to do. He continued to travel and tell others about Jesus.

David knew that God had work for him to do.

Even though he felt lonely David knew that he was not alone. David knew that God was with him. Even though he was sad, David knew that one day he would meet Jesus face to face and that would be perfect. Even though he was in danger, David knew that God was stronger than his enemies, stronger even than death. David knew that God is the strongest and the bravest.

David knew this as he knelt down in his little hut by the Zambezi River. It was time to pray to God. And it was then that God took David home to heaven just as he had promised.

David knew that God is the strongest and the bravest.

© Copyright 2008 Catherine Mackenzie
Reprinted in 2012
Written with love for my sisters Marianne and Wilma
ISBN: 978-1-84550-384-0

Published by Christian Focus Publications
Geanies House, Fearn, Tain, Ross-shire, IV20 1TW, Scotland, U.K.
www.christianfocus.com
Illustrated by Rita Ammassari
Cover design by Daniel van Straaten
Printed in China

Other titles in this series:
Corrie ten Boom: Are all of the watches safe? 978-1-84550-109-9
Amy Carmichael: Can brown eyes be made blue? 978-1-84550-108-2
Hudson Taylor: Could somebody pass the salt? 978-1-84550-111-2
George Müller: Does money grow on trees? 978-1-84550-110-5
Helen Roseveare: What's in the Parcel? 978-1-84550-383-3